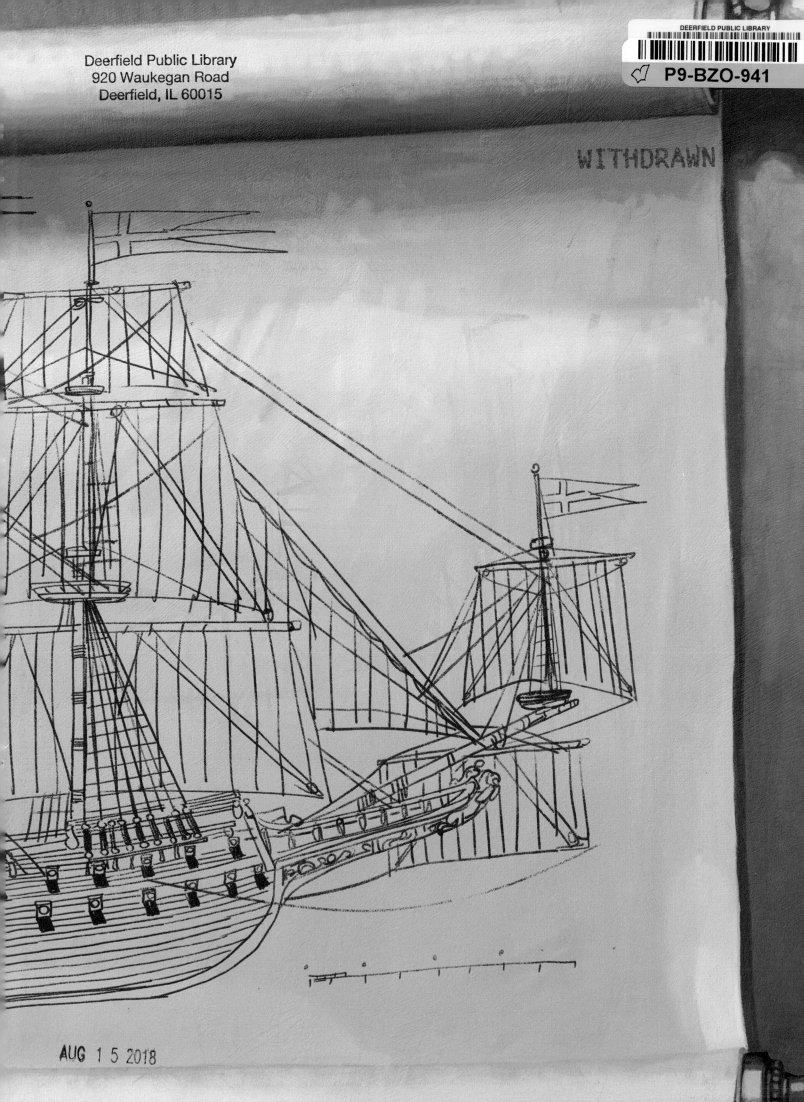

*To the unsinkable Dana Jagelski*

*—R. F.*

*To Russell Freedman*

*—W. L.*

Henry Holt and Company, *Publishers since 1866*
Henry Holt® is a registered trademark of Macmillan Publishing Group, LLC
175 Fifth Avenue, New York, NY 10010 • mackids.com

Text copyright © 2018 by Russell Freedman
Illustrations copyright © 2018 by William Low
All rights reserved.

ISBN 978-1-62779-866-2
Library of Congress Control Number 2017957923

Our books may be purchased in bulk for promotional, educational, or business use. Please
contact your local bookseller or the Macmillan Corporate and Premium Sales Department at
(800) 221-7945 ext. 5442 or by e-mail at MacmillanSpecialMarkets@macmillan.com.

First edition, 2018 / Design by Patrick Collins
The artist used Adobe Photoshop and Adobe Illustrator to create the art for this book.
Printed in China by RR Donnelley Asia Printing Solutions Ltd., Dongguan City, Guangdong Province

10 9 8 7 6 5 4 3 2 1

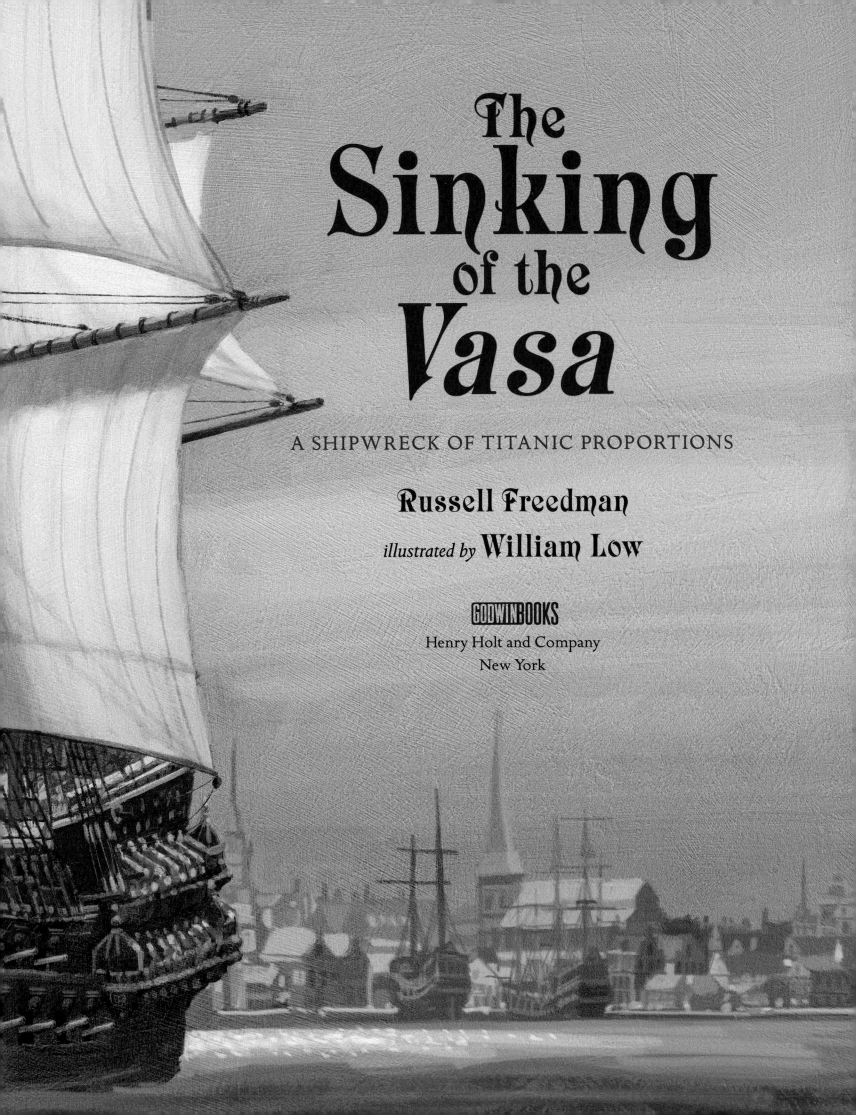

# The Sinking of the Vasa

## A SHIPWRECK OF TITANIC PROPORTIONS

### Russell Freedman

*illustrated by* **William Low**

**GODWINBOOKS**

Henry Holt and Company
New York

THE KING OF SWEDEN HAD SPOKEN. At his command, an army of loggers marched into the forest and cut down a thousand giant oaks. The lumber was piled onto barges, then floated to the navy shipyard in Stockholm.

King Gustav II Adolf had ordered the construction of the mightiest warship the world had ever seen—a vessel so fearsome, the very sight of her would shiver the timbers of any enemy ship.

Four hundred craftsmen skilled in the art of shipbuilding labored for more than two years before the king's new warship was ready to be launched.

King Gustav visited the shipyard to inspect the vessel. He announced that she would be named the *Vasa*, after the house of Vasa, the family that sat on the Swedish throne. Sweden was a maritime superpower, often at war with her neighbors. The *Vasa* would be the navy's pride and a symbol of Gustav's wealth and prestige.

Designed to terrify enemies and dazzle everyone who saw her, the *Vasa* was almost as long as a city block. Her soaring masts, as tall as a fourteen-story building, could support ten billowing white sails. Gun decks on either side of the ship could hold sixty-four bronze cannons. They could fire a broadside that would blow an enemy ship out of the water.

An imposing machine of war, the *Vasa* was a work of art as well, a wonder to behold. Hundreds of painted and gilded sculptures and carvings—angels and devils, warriors and musicians, mermaids, emperors and gods—decorated her richly ornamented hull.

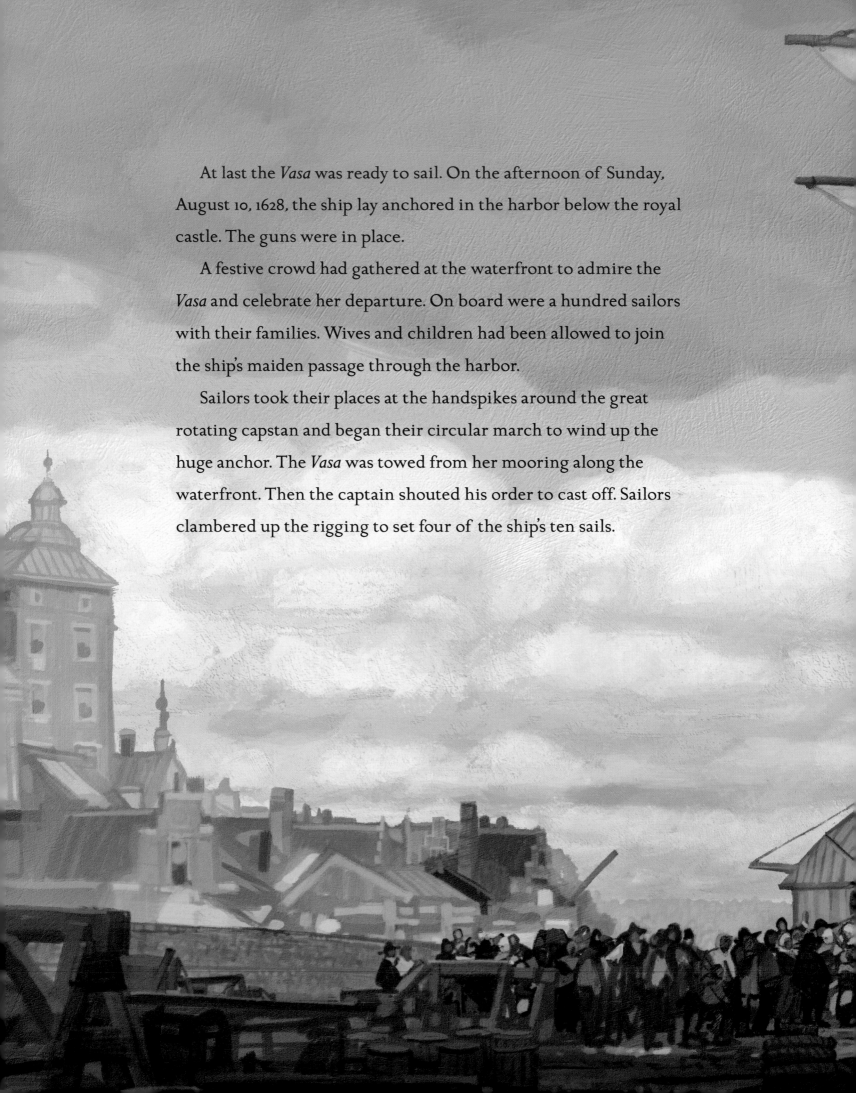

At last the *Vasa* was ready to sail. On the afternoon of Sunday, August 10, 1628, the ship lay anchored in the harbor below the royal castle. The guns were in place.

A festive crowd had gathered at the waterfront to admire the *Vasa* and celebrate her departure. On board were a hundred sailors with their families. Wives and children had been allowed to join the ship's maiden passage through the harbor.

Sailors took their places at the handspikes around the great rotating capstan and began their circular march to wind up the huge anchor. The *Vasa* was towed from her mooring along the waterfront. Then the captain shouted his order to cast off. Sailors clambered up the rigging to set four of the ship's ten sails.

The sails caught the breeze, and the *Vasa* moved grandly through the harbor on her own. Small boats followed in the ship's wake, the people on them waving and shouting "Good luck!" and "Farewell!"

A gust of wind caught the ship's sails. The *Vasa* heeled sharply, leaning to one side, then righted herself. The captain ordered all crewmen to their stations.

Struck by another wind gust, stronger than the first, the ship again heeled over, even farther. This time, water gushed through the open gunports. A moment later, the ship's deck railings were slapping against the waves, then disappearing underwater.

With flags flying, the mighty warship began to sink. She had traveled barely 1,300 meters—not even a mile.

Crewmen with their wives and children threw themselves into the water and swam for their lives. Some clung to the rigging as the ship went under, crying out for help. Small boats rushed to the scene and rescued all they could reach. But not everyone could be saved.

How could this disaster have befallen the pride of the Swedish navy? How could such a catastrophe take place as the good citizens of Stockholm looked on in horror and disbelief? Why did the *Vasa* sink? And who was to blame?

All over the kingdom, people grieved for those who had been lost. They congregated in the streets and squares, taverns and inns, to talk endlessly about the terrible accident.

King Gustav ordered an investigation. Those responsible for the sinking had to be punished! The *Vasa*'s captain had been arrested and questioned at the castle. Had he failed to make sure that the guns were properly secured? Had he been drinking that day? Was he, in fact, drunk when the *Vasa* keeled over and sank?

"You can cut me into a thousand pieces if the guns were not secured," Captain Söfring Hansson protested. "And before God Almighty I swear that no one on board was intoxicated."

The captain blamed the ship's design for the disaster. And for the faulty design, he blamed the shipbuilder. "The ship was too unsteady," he argued. "It was just a small gust of wind, a mere breeze, that overturned the *Vasa*."

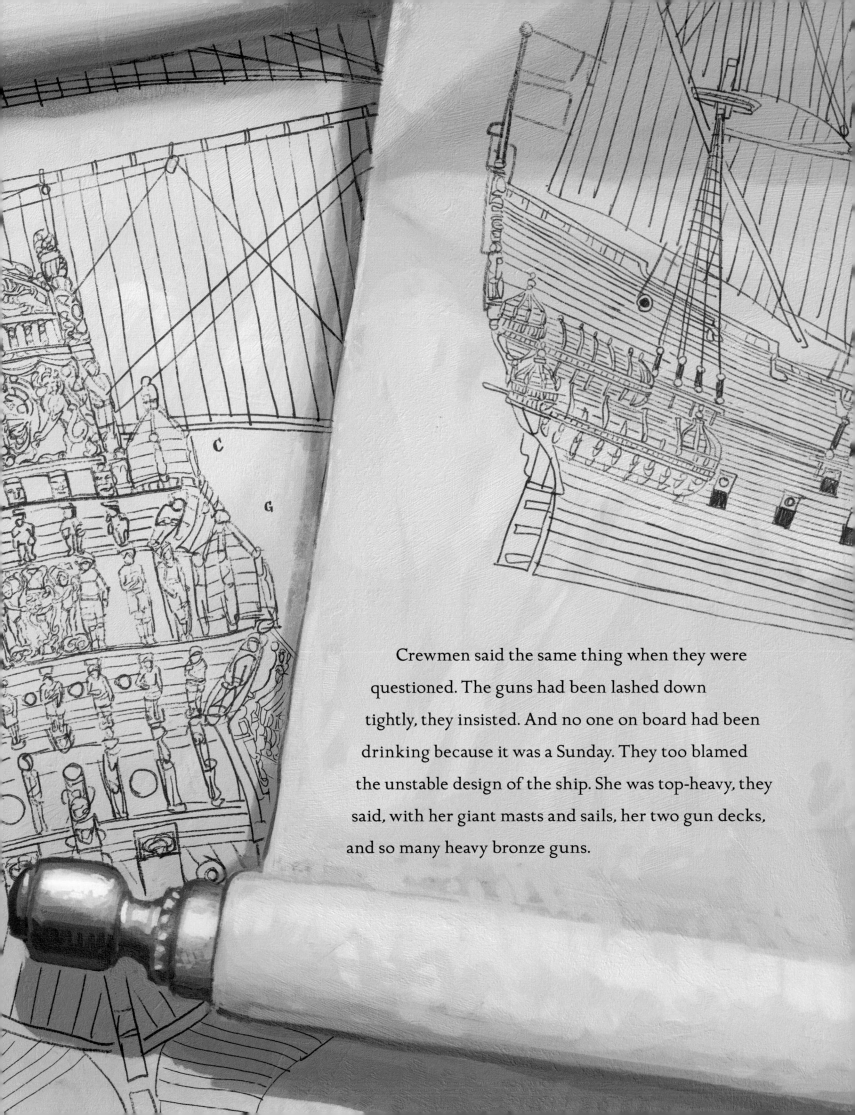

Crewmen said the same thing when they were questioned. The guns had been lashed down tightly, they insisted. And no one on board had been drinking because it was a Sunday. They too blamed the unstable design of the ship. She was top-heavy, they said, with her giant masts and sails, her two gun decks, and so many heavy bronze guns.

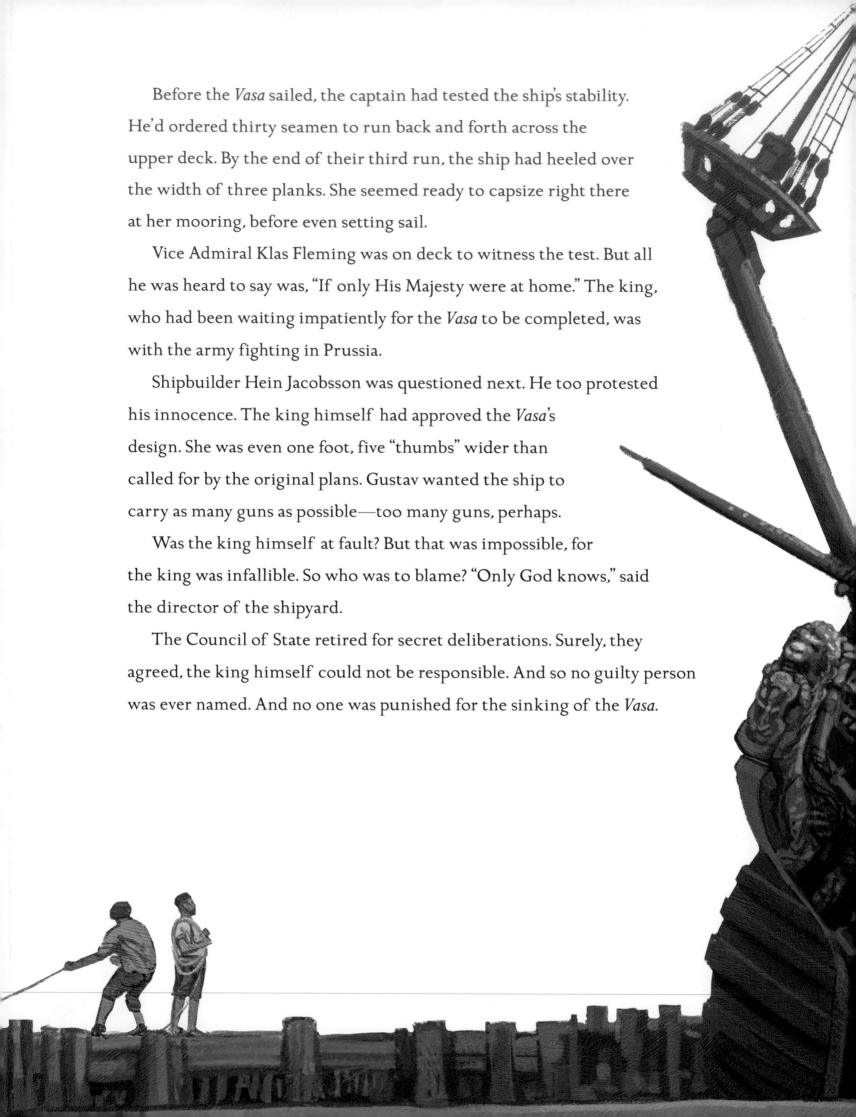

Before the *Vasa* sailed, the captain had tested the ship's stability. He'd ordered thirty seamen to run back and forth across the upper deck. By the end of their third run, the ship had heeled over the width of three planks. She seemed ready to capsize right there at her mooring, before even setting sail.

Vice Admiral Klas Fleming was on deck to witness the test. But all he was heard to say was, "If only His Majesty were at home." The king, who had been waiting impatiently for the *Vasa* to be completed, was with the army fighting in Prussia.

Shipbuilder Hein Jacobsson was questioned next. He too protested his innocence. The king himself had approved the *Vasa*'s design. She was even one foot, five "thumbs" wider than called for by the original plans. Gustav wanted the ship to carry as many guns as possible—too many guns, perhaps.

Was the king himself at fault? But that was impossible, for the king was infallible. So who was to blame? "Only God knows," said the director of the shipyard.

The Council of State retired for secret deliberations. Surely, they agreed, the king himself could not be responsible. And so no guilty person was ever named. And no one was punished for the sinking of the *Vasa*.

The *Vasa* lay at the bottom of the
harbor, her rigging a playground for fish,
her sails waving lazily with the currents,
her body littered with the skeletons
of those who had perished.

with meat, reduced to bones, lay in the hold. Two wooden butter casks contained 333-year-old butter. The ship's oaken hull, blackened by so much time underwater, was still sturdy, and she was able to float unaided. The *Vasa* was towed to a dry dock not far from where she had sunk.

The first to board were Anders Franzén, who had discovered the wreck, and Per Edvin Fälting, the diver who first reached out to touch the ship. The two men stepped aboard. They shook hands. Then they tossed a good-luck coin onto the *Vasa*'s deck.

Years of restoration work followed. The first year, the *Vasa*'s waterlogged oaken hull was sprayed daily with cold water to clean it and prevent it from shrinking and cracking. Then a preservative was sprayed daily for another seventeen years. Parts of the ship were reconstructed. Skilled craftsmen reassembled thousands of loose objects rescued during the salvaging operation. The three masts, pieced back together by carpenters, were reattached to the hull.

Rigging that had been destroyed was replaced. Wood carvers and painters cleaned, repaired, and repainted the hundreds of sculptures decorating the *Vasa*'s hull. Gradually the ship was transformed from a wreck and rebuilt until she began to look like herself again.

Today the restored ship sits grandly on display at the Stockholm museum built especially to house her. She can be seen as she would have looked in 1628 while laid up in port for the winter, with her three lower masts and rigging in place and her upper masts in winter storage. She has become one of the most popular tourist attractions in Sweden, admired by millions of visitors from all over the world.

Sweden today is a proud nation that has long been at peace. The Nobel Peace Prize was created by the Swedish explosives manufacturer Alfred Nobel.

Three of the *Vasa*'s original bronze cannons were recovered, preserved, and replaced in their gunports. Meant to destroy enemy ships, they instead helped topple and sink the doomed *Vasa*. To this day, they have never fired a shot. In their silence lies a king's misguided dream of military might. And the *Vasa*, in her restored glory, is herself a testament to peace.

## SOURCES

Cederlund, Carl Olof. *Vasa I: The Archaeology of a Swedish Royal Ship of 1628*. Stockholm: National Maritime Museum of Sweden, 2006.

Dupuy, Trevor Nevitt. *The Military Life of Gustavus Adolphus*. New York: Franklin Watts, 1969.

Hocker, Frederick M. *Vasa: A Swedish Warship*. Stockholm: Medstroms Bokforlag, 2011.

Kvarning, Lars-Ake, and Bengt Ohrelius. *The Vasa: The Royal Ship*. Stockholm: Atlantis Bokforlag, 1998.

Matz, Erling. *Vasa 1628*. Stockholm: Vasa Museum, 1990.

Roberts, Michael, ed. *Sweden as a Great Power 1611–1697*. London: St. Martin's Press, 1968.

The Vasa Museum, vasamuseet.se/en

*The Warship Vasa*, directed and edited by Anders Wahlgren. Vasa Museum, 2007, DVD.